Wife of an Angel
WOUNDS THIS DEEP

Copyright © 2020 by G.Kaur

All rights reserved. This book or any portion thereof may not be reproduced or used in any manner whatsoever without the express written permission of the publisher except for the use of brief quotations in a book review.

ISBN 978-1-7107-4377-7

Dedication

This book is dedicated to my best friend, my late husband M.S.G. and to all those who have lost someone dear to their hearts. I miss you dearly and I love you more than anything.

I never knew what love was
till you came into my life,
I never knew such sadness
could exist till you left,
And now alone,
Here I remain
an Angel's Wife.

Dancing with grief,
Is something I do everyday,
Sometimes I make it through
the steps in sequence,
And other times I leap and
spin and sway back and forth,
Denial, Anger,
Bargaining, Depression,
And lastly Acceptance, which by
far is the hardest to process,
My mind quickly jumps back
to Denial, to make it hurt less,
Dancing with grief,
a recital without an end.

Today is the present.
Since the day you left,
a gift I never wanted.

Where you have gone
is where I long to be,
Because without you here,
I feel empty,
I do not need
this world anymore,
Will you please come
show me the door?

King of my heart,
From you, I never wanted to be apart,
My heart has turned into stone,
How could this be something
God could condone?
Could he not see how much
I love you,
Could he not see how much
I need you,
My soul, it cries out in pain,
It will continue to do so
till we meet again.

Any torture imaginable
would be less painful
than living another day
without you.

I cry myself to sleep each night,
Without you here, nothing is right,
I wish I would not wake up to see
another day,
For us to be reunited is the only
thing for which I pray.

All I feel is empty.

I have been gutted
like a fish with a knife,
Why shall I carry on,
so pointless is this life,
This unbearable sadness
hurts me physically,
You will never be here,
is something I fail
to understand mentally.

I just have to believe
that you are somewhere better,
Because this is Hell
I am living in
without you,
I just have to believe you
are somewhere better,
That is what I pray for,
for it is all I can do.

I will love you always,
Love you for all of my days,
Even though you have
gone so far away,
I will always hold you in my heart,
Even though you are not here,
To me, you will always
be the most dear.

Like a song without a beat,

Without you,

I am incomplete.

I do not know how
I am still breathing,
I do not know how
my heart is still beating,
If you take a closer look,
you will see my heart is
broken beyond repair,
My whole life, with
you I wanted to share,
You are gone,
how can it be true,
You are gone,
now what am I to do?

I always wonder if you can see
and hear me from wherever you are,
I pray for you each night on a
twinkling star,
I hope you know that from my heart
you will never be far,
Please remember to save me a spot,
right next to you, wherever you are.

Pulseless;
without a heart,
When God took you,
He tore it out
and ripped it apart.

Empty;

I am hollow,

Just reach out

and give me your hand,

Oh my love,

without hesitation

I will follow.

Every breath I take,
I wish would be my last,
There is nothing left
in this world for me,
My heart cries
knowing you will only
be in my past.

They say home is
where the heart is,
Honey, you took
that with you,
So, my home is
where you are,
Darling, you know
that is true.

My arms long to hold you,
My hands long to touch you,
My heart aches in pain without you,
My eyes weep because
they can no longer see you.

How can the sun continue to shine?
When the only thing of value is
gone from this life of mine.
I ask how is this possible,
How could this be,
it is just not rational.

I still visit
the places
we used to go,
hoping that
I will find
you there.

Memories of you,
Memories of us,
They are so bittersweet.
First I smile,
for I was so lucky to have you,
And then hits a tidal wave of despair,
I have lost everything;
You are no longer here.

As another tear falls from my eyes,
How much I love you,
I hope God can see and realize,
He should not have taken you alone,
I sit here wondering why this happened,
Why are you gone,
My heart may be beating,
And I may be breathing,
But without you, I am dead inside,
Oh God, will you not take me as well?
I long to be by his side.

Darkness fell,
The world stood
silent and still,
Full of rage,
Full of sadness,
To go on,
I have no will.

I may as well be a magician,
By the wave of a wand I create
and make you believe in fallacy,
For the me that I am now,
The me that I allow you to see,
Is but just an illusion of
who I used to be.

There is not a moment of the
day that I do not think of you,
Not a moment that I do not
wonder what we would be doing,
If only you were here with me too.

If only, life came with a remote.
I would rewind back to the
moments I had with you,
and live in them forever.

If I could have made a deal with
God to take the years I have
left to live and give half to you,
I would not have hesitated for
even a fraction of a second,
Because, pointless is this life
I am living without you.

Everyday,

I am consumed by thoughts of you,

The depth of my love,

I hope you know,

My heart will forever belong to you,

This is for certain;

it will always be true.

On most days you
made me feel like
I was your Sun,
It was I, you said,
who brought light
into your world,
I never got the
chance to tell you,
So I hope you know,
I hope you knew,
You are my
whole damn Universe.

I am dumbfounded when
people tell me,
"Despite it all, you are
doing pretty good,"
But they do not know the
chaos that is within me,
To comprehend my pain,
They never could.

My world has turned dark and cold,
Everyday I live is yet another torture,
You and I, together, we were
supposed to grow old.

My heart breaks daily and the tears
flee from my eyes,
It is the worst when I wake up
without you knowing I will have to
live another day alone,
It is the worst when I go to sleep
without you at night and realize
another day has passed by
since you left,
And it is the worst during the
time in between.

I would have never
let you go,
If it were up to me,
For you are the only love
I knew,
The only love
I will ever know.

Day turns to night,
Night turns to day,
Nothing changes,
Yet nothing is the same.

Although I know you have gone,
I still cannot fathom the thought of
living the rest of my life without you,
Each time my mind begins to think about it,
I find myself breathless,
gasping for air, on my knees.

On the outside

I may seem as if I am fine,

On the inside

I am battered, bruised and blue,

Parts of me are broken

and bleeding

that I never even knew.

Full of Rage,
I see through crimson glass,
I want to set the world on fire,
Sit and watch everything burn,
This world has taken
everything from me,
I want revenge, when will
it be my turn.

I never knew I could feel this lonely,
I always thought loneliness was
something that was felt only
when you were alone,
Now
I can admit that I was wrong,
I feel it always,
When I am with others
and when I am all alone.

When I promised you forever,
My promise was true,
Is true,
Will forever be true,
For I will always want and
need only you,
Never was there nor
will there ever be,
Someone who could
ever compare to thee.

There is nothing

I would not

offer to God

in exchange

for you.

This Earth
was not meant to witness us for long,
Our love was more than
it could handle;
Our love was just too strong,
In this universe there must be a place
that exists where together we can be,
A place where we can have our
forever finally,
And I know when I find it,
you will be there waiting for me.

Waking up and living
without you is the cruelest
torture I have ever had to
endure,
This grief has dug its claws
deep within me and
has taken over,
There is no remedy to fix me,
Sweet death is the only
cure.

They say true love
knows no end,
I am just waiting
to receive my wings,
So, to you I can
ascend.

I never knew it would
be this hard to breathe,
I touch and smell the
clothes you used to wear,
I try to find a trace of your scent,
Then I find myself choking on tears,
I am suffocating,
I fall down to my knees,
This facade, this disguise I wear,
is quite deceiving for you cannot
see what rots underneath.

And because you have gone,
In this lifetime I will die twice,
I have died once,
Now, I wait only to die again.

My heart is broken
yet it still pumps
blood through my veins,
I am without hope,
Another day goes by,
and still no one can
understand my pains.

Life is a collection of moments,
the best ones are those which
I had with you.

We vanished.
I can no longer see you,
And I do not recognize
the person who looks
back at me in the mirror.

Everlasting

Is my love for you,

No matter where I am,

No matter where I go,

My love for you

will know no end.

Grief.

It is not a straight path,

It comes in cycles like the tide,

Some waves are barely bearable,

And others so strong they

take me under,

I find myself drowning,

I see a light,

Then all of a sudden I wash

up upon shore,

I have to force myself up and

stand up to the tide once more.

My existence is now divided into two,
One part is with, the other
without you,
I will never be the same,
This life I have learned is nothing but
a cruel, unfair game.

The only thing that
keeps me going,
Is the thought that
rivers keep flowing,
But one day, they
reach their destination,
they reach the shore,
To get to where you are
that is all I am praying for,
In this life I have never
wanted anything more.

And I can still feel your presence
through the warmth of the suns rays,
And with each drop of rain,
I can still hear you when the
wind rustles through the crisp leaves,
And the sweet songs the birds sing,
You will always be with me,
I know that for certain even
though you I cannot see,
For if it were up to you,
you would have never left me.

Simply speaking,
My eyes will never again see
what they are always seeking.

You and I,
Our love is like that which
is between the sun and the moon,
They may never be together,
Yet their love lights up the sky.

In so much pain,
I am going numb,
Everything I have lost,
These wounds are too deep,
I wish to succumb.

You were taken too early,
Now I cannot clearly see,
In a blur, in a haze,
Imprisoned by life,
for the remainder of
my days.

With great love,
Comes great grief,
Comes greater pain,
Devours all of you,
There is no relief.

They say a dream
is a wish your heart makes,
That must certainly be true,
Because when I dream,
I dream only of you.

Pretending like I am okay,
I am so close to the edge,
I wear a mask for the world,
Hopeless;
I might as well walk off the ledge.

Against all odds we came together,
Thought we would be forever, You and I.
The day God called upon you was the
start of my darkest, coldest days,
Slowly dying like the Earth would be
without the warmth of the suns rays.
We are no longer together, You and I.
Surrounded by people,
Yet I remain the loneliest of souls,
Without you, I can never be whole.
I await the day when I can join you,
And in the end, again it will be You and I.

Turmoil inside me,
So immense is this pain,
Leaves me with no place to hide,
Drowns me like monsoon rain.

Down for the count,
This life has knocked me out,
Silently crying in pain and agony,
I am alone,
No one can hear my soul
scream and shout.

Our love was like a fairytale,
You were so handsome,
So charming, for real.
More than life itself,
I love you,
I would give anything
to be with you,
You were the reason for all my
Smiles and laughter,
I wonder why we got dealt
this tragedy,
All I wanted was
a happily ever after.

Time was not on our side,
We simply did not have enough,
We thought we had so much more,
Father Time's pokerface
was too convincing,
I wish I could have called his bluff.

You were the sole reason,
Love was something
I could believe in,
Now, you are gone
and I am all alone,
Withering away,
Waiting to for the curtain
to close and someone to say
"la fin."

My reality,

It is now but

an endless nightmare,

Wish I could wake up,

It is just not fair.

I think of you,

Tears roll down my face,

I cannot breathe,

My heart begins to race,

They tell me it will

get better with time,

I know that is not the case,

Because together we were like music,

I was the treble and you,

the bass.

Since the day you left,
I just want to die,
My soul continues to cry,
I cry for the tomorrows
we were supposed to have,
The places we would see,
I cry for how our life
together was supposed to be,
God was just too selfish,
just too unkind,
He took my love from
me and left me behind.

When you touched me,
I felt your touch upon my skin,
But your fingerprints were
permanently left etched upon my soul.

I often think of the memories
we made so very fondly,
But each time I think of you,
the wind gets knocked out of me.

If I could capture all my tears,
There would be enough to make
an ocean or a sea,
I would set sail to find you,
From this world I would flee.

Darkness has surrounded me,
Engulfed me entirely,
To breath is difficult, to live
without you unbearable,
There is no way anyone
can understand,
The pain is incomparable.

My heart bleeds, my soul is
drowning in sorrow,
Stuck in the midst of this misery,
How I wish this was not reality,
Wish I could go to sleep and wake
up next to you magically,
But, alas, I know that cannot be,
So, as I lay my head down each night,
I pray I will not wake up to see
another tomorrow.

Your love,

it resonates within,

Your touch,

it is tattooed on my skin,

All the memories of you

I will cherish forever,

And we will make more,

when we are once again

together.

Beaten by life,
It has left me
black and blue,
Broken.
Bruised.
Bleeding.
I do not need saving,
Just come back
and take me with you.

I never imagined that
life would be like this,
I never thought I would have
to wake up without your kiss,
I am left here not sure
what to believe in,
I do not have the strength
to go on within.

Thoughts race through my mind,
Yet I am at a loss for words,
I sit here silently,
I never knew my kismet
would bring me to my knees.

I sit here wondering was
this some kind of cruel joke,
Was this some kind of test,
Did God break my heart
to prove that he only
takes the best?

In the game of chess,
The Queen protects the King,
I wish I could have saved you,
I would have sacrificed myself,
Just as a candle burns
itself to give light.

To live this life without you
is something I cannot fathom,
To know this is my reality
makes my whole body numb.

I wish I had you close,
I wish I could have you near,
Because when you were with me,
I had nothing to fear,
You are My King, My Lion,
So fierce and so strong,
Beside you, is where I belong.

It is not raining,

Though you may

see drops of rain,

The angels are

crying, for we

are apart,

And my soul

bleeds for

you in pain.

If I could make one wish,
I would wish for you,
Wish this nightmare was not true,
The love I have for you
is beyond measure,
You will forever be
my one and only treasure.

I ask you all these questions, But you don't ever seem to hear,

I keep asking for answers, This pain is too much to bear,

They tell me it is temporary, They tell me this too shall pass,

Just like the cold winter snaps of January,

Float away, in the summer, like dandelions in the grass,

Perhaps you don't have answers, That is why you stay quiet,

You only take those you want, And no one can dare defy it,

As for the saying, all wounds time will heal,

Unfortunate fools are those who say that, for they never had a love so real.

Denial is a crutch that helps us grieve,
It becomes something we
use when the truth we do
not want to believe,
It is a crutch that I now
use quite often,
Although it helps sometimes, the
stone my heart has become it will
never soften.

A story that is told,
Becomes a story to tell,
Some tell it beautifully, so well,
Some stories are so moving they
lift your spirit high,
Some stories are filled with so
much sorrow they make you cry,
Our story,
once as radiant as could be,
In the end
became a heartbreaking tragedy.

I have often heard that
Heaven is beautiful,
Now I know that
is surely true,
Because Heaven
has the most
perfect angel,
You.

I always thought I was quite
good at the game of hide and seek,
You have clearly proved me wrong,
Because where you have gone to hide,
I will spend the rest of my
life trying to seek.

I long to see your smile,
Your beautiful face, the
twinkle in your eyes,
I know it has only been
awhile but with each
sunrise a part of me dies,
Since you have gone, it
feels like it has been an eternity,
I only wish to hold you
close and feel your warmth
around me.

A prisoner of this world,
I am in shackles and chains,
My heart aches, my soul cries
out in pain,
Won't you come give me the key,
Come set me free,
So I can be with you,
There is no place
I would rather be.

For what is the purpose,
What do I have to live for?
My dreams and aspirations shattered,
I do not need this life anymore,
I scream "God will you not take
pity upon my soul,
Take away this pain, reunite me
with him and make me whole."

They say time is the answer,
All wounds it will heal,
That is a pile of rubbish,
For nothing will ever fill
your void, nothing will ever
change the way I feel.

I do not think
about the future,
I do not think
about tomorrow,
Surviving even the very
next minute is already
more than I can handle.

All they do is ask if I am okay,
I say I am fine, but if I were to tell
the truth the answer will always be no,
How can I be fine when I
feel completely empty inside,
I just want to run away,
never to be seen again,
All I want to do is hide.

Happiness is but a memory.

Now, something I will never feel,
Without you it will never truly be real,
Without you I will always be blue,
Perhaps a different shade
perhaps a different hue,
Because happiness, for me,
existed only when I was
with you.

Since the day God held
your hand and took you away,
The colours of my life
have washed away,
Like an old movie reel,
my world is now monochromatic;
black and white,
And without you,
nothing will ever be right.

The tide has come in
and has washed me away,
I cannot swim nor surface for air,
My lungs fill with water,
I descend into the deep sea,
I must surrender to my despair.

The spaces between my fingers,
Were always meant for yours,
For this life and for all of eternity,
You will always be mi amor.

No longer may I be able to
feel you with my hands,
But I will feel you always
with each beat of my heart.

Like flowers in a garden,
My love blooms for you,
It will continue to grow,
My love for you will never die,
For I water it everyday
with the tears I cry.

I had found
my home in
your arms,
And since
you have gone,
I wander
through the
days in agony for now
I am homeless.

As you look down upon
me from Heaven,
I hope you can hear,
All the things I say aloud,
And all the things my heart says
silently which end with tears.

They ask me if I am all right,
I reply that I am okay,
Deep inside of me,
I know nothing is right,
I do not know how
long I can keep lying,
I cannot fake it everyday,
I am slowly dying,
Death is the only answer
to take my pain away.

After God took you,

My life was divided into two,

In one part we both existed,

Now,

Neither of us do.

I still remember the last time
I felt your lips upon mine,
Oh, how badly I wish I could
turn back the hands of time.

Broken.

My heart is shattered,

Damaged beyond repair,

I try to get through another day,

On the outside I may look fine,

Guess it is quite convincing,

this mask I wear,

Inside, it is another story,

A true juxtaposition,

I am drowning in

despair.

No one can truly see,

What your absence has done to me,

I just want to run to some

place far away,

Wish I could find you along the way.

I will wait a thousand lifetimes,
And I will wait a thousand more,
I will wait however long
it takes to find you,
Because you are the only one
worth waiting for.

If silence truly does
utter a thousand words,
What my soul screams,
Even a word, have you heard?

They say there is a
light at the end of the tunnel,
But in a tunnel I am not, I never was,
I am in a bottomless hole
and I keep falling deeper and deeper,
Becoming progressively
darker and more cold,
This is my grief,
What I feel cannot be
expressed in words to be told.

I wander aimlessly
through the day,
Lay sleepless
through the night,
I think of you
constantly,
I wonder why
did God serve
us this plight.

I wear your clothes sometimes,
For it is the only way I can feel a
heart beat underneath them now.

Soul mates exist.

I am certain you are mine,

Although we are apart,

We will be reunited come the right time,

My souls final destination is

wherever you are.

I have never
felt so lonely,
So lonely
I have never felt,
Whether I am alone
Or
Sitting in a
crowded room,
I am lonely,
The loneliest
I have ever felt.

Your presence consumed me,
Your absence consumes me still,
In awe of you I was,
Be mesmerized by you,
I always will.

I always see you
with my eyes closed,
I just wish I could
see you with them open.

I know you are waiting for me,
Just as I am waiting to be with you,
This tortuous thing we call life is
just something I have to get through.

I close my eyes
and it is you I see,
I dream of you and I nightly,
I wish I could stay asleep
for the rest of my life,
For my dreams will always be
better than my reality.

Since you are gone,
There is no reason for
my heart to beat,
Or for me to remain here without you,
Life is unknowingly a war;
I surrender,
I accept defeat.

I only miss you

with each breath I take

and

with each beat of my heart.

The only peace I will ever know
is the first few seconds when I awake,
That is the only time I do not
remember from me, what God did take,
I wonder why this decision was one
he had to make,
Because if it was my loves choice,
me, he would never forsake.

The greatest pain is
to live without you,
Nothing will ever
lessen this pain,
Like a shadow
which always follows,
It is just something
I have to live with.

If I could follow
my heart,
I would end
up right there
beside you.

They say I need to be strong,
In time things will get better,
These are nothing but spoken words,
For I know, you cannot
imagine the storm that
brews inside of me,
I know these words
you would not dare utter,
If only they had to walk
a day in these shoes of mine.

The stars they shine brighter,
For they are competing with you,
You will always be the one that shines
the brightest,
The brightest star in my sky will
always be you.

I once was lost,
You walked into my life
and I was found,
Now you are gone,
you have left never to return,
And I remain here, a corpse
walking above ground.

Darkness falls,

In the sky stars appear,

Memories of you

make me feel warm,

Then comes a tear.

Every time I close my eyes
I see your handsome face,
Wish I could have your arms
Around me in sweet embrace,
I would hold you so tight,
never let you get away,
Because I need you
here with me each
and every day,
Won't you come
and take me away?

And some days
I am unable to face the world,
So I hide under the covers
and let the tears freely flow.

The ocean could never
be more blue,
Just as our love could
never be more true,
Love was something,
before you, I never knew,
You have gone and
I await the day I can
bid this world adieu.

The distance
between
us may
be infinite,
Just as
my love
for you.

Because of You,
I believed that
Dreams could
come true,
Then Life
showed me,
Nightmares
can too.

I love you
with all of me,
I will grieve for
you the same,
I have heard
grief is love
with just a
different name.

Because I now
live in Hell,
There is a fire so
fierce that burns
within me,
It will incinerate
anyone who
comes too close.

In these times
they say it is
rare to find
a love that is
true,
Those who say that
never did know me
nor did they know
you,
For we loved with a love
that could not possibly
be more true.

Misery

Has befriended me,

Her nails have dug into

my skin, she has latched on,

Alone, she will never let me be,

She will stay by my side,

She will torment me mercilessly,

I await the day Death comes

Only then will I be set

free.

The day I lost you,
I lost myself as well,
Stuck in a dark abyss,
Now all I do is reminisce.

The depth of
my wounds
get deeper
with each
passing day,
This pain, I know,
is here to stay,
Until my last breath,
Until the last beat
of my heart,
Until then,
this pain will
not go away.

The day I stop missing
you will be the day
my heart stops beating.

All I am waiting for
is the final curtain call,
For my end will be near,
I will be smiling,
For soon I will again be with you,
You are all I ever need,
Other than you,
I do not need anything at all.

I am waiting for the place

where forever exists for us.

How do I make my poor heart understand the fact that you will never be coming home to me?

My mind does not even want to acknowledge this cruel truth,

In the morning I awake without you and my mind tries to make me believe that you have gone to work,

As the day draws to an end, night falls and I am without you still,

That is when my mind can no longer make me believe a lie and I know,

I am living my nightmare…

For you will never be coming home to me.

The love you gave
me in this life
is enough to
last till we
meet again.

As time passes,
I have learned that it is easier
to be fake and say I'm fine,
As time passes,
I have learned this grief that
kills me everyday,
It will never change,
As time passes,
I have learned it will
never be as things were,
nothing will ever
be the same.

Fall turns to winter,
The days turn dark and cold,
So lonely am I,
You are the only one
my arms long to hold.

If only I could find a way to you,
There is nothing I would not do,
I would leave no place left to look,
Our love was magical,
like a tale out of a book,
Every minute I am awake,
I ask how could this be true,
God must have needed a
perfect angel, so he took you,
All I hope is one day soon,
he will take me too.

I would trade all
my tomorrows,
To be with you,
If I could do that my
only wish could come true,
For all my tomorrows
would also be
with you too.

I am fearless,
For I am no longer afraid,
Fear itself can fear me,
For nothing can ever
give me more pain
than your absence.

My heart is
broken into so
many pieces,
but for you it
will always sing,
I love you,
I love you
more than
anything.

These tears that fall
from my eyes fall
because I have lost you,
Last night, just like every
night, they fell too,
This heartache is here to
stay, it will never go away,
We are inseparable: like my
shadow it will follow me everyday.

Out of all the music in the world,
my favourite was the beat
I could hear when I rested
my head upon your chest.

This grief is a monster,
He feeds on me everyday,
I sit here while he
takes another bite,
He never leaves,
He is always near,
Always in my sight,
There is no way of
escaping him
Too tired,
I give up,
I will not fight.

No, I do not
remember you.
To remember
is to once have
forgotten,
How can I
remember you
if you never
leave my mind.

You were stolen, Stolen from me,

God let it happen, How did he let it be?

What am I left to believe in? Faith?

I'm questioning it,

for what good did that do me?

Others repeatedly tell me that things happen
for a reason, someone care to explain?

Why was he chosen to depart, why was I
chosen to carry so much pain?

Why do the good ones suffer,

Why do they get taken so young?

Please someone, someone please explain,
why all of a sudden can you not talk?

Why do you have a twisted tongue?

You never know the
value of memories
until
the memories are
all you have left.

I reach out my arms as far as I can,
Would you just take my hand,
All I want is all I need,
That is you, do you understand?
I reach out my arms,
Darling just take my hand,
This is not where I belong,
Without you, this is a strange,
unfamiliar land.

A shattered heart can still function,
I am, unfortunately, living proof of it,
Although I wish it had stopped
beating at the same time yours did.

Like a name written in sand,
The waves have washed you away,
I have written my name as well,
I am just waiting for that sweet day
when I too will be a memory of yesterday.

Perhaps this was not our time,
Perhaps this was not our place,
But I have to believe that
sometime, somewhere
we will be able to be.

Your absence

is felt

through the

emptiness

inside

every part

of me.

I stare out my window,
Watch day turn to night,
You have gone so far away,
So far away, out out of sight,
Until we meet again I will
keep you in my heart,
Safe and tucked in so tight.

There is no one
here who can wipe
away my tears,
Nor is there
anyone who can
stop them from
falling,
I sit quietly,
I do not say
a word,
But for you, my
heart is always calling.

With the pieces of half a puzzle we are born,

The other half are in the hands of our soul mate,

We roam this world incomplete until we find him or her by fate,

The pieces fit so perfectly,

To reveal a masterpiece, a true sight to see,

Our pieces had fit together just the same,

All of a sudden you have vanished,

All of your pieces are gone too,

I am still here,

With the pieces to half our beautiful puzzle, now damaged, tarnished and torn.

My eyes are swollen,
My cheeks are wet,
I have had enough of this torture,
Why isn't my life over yet?

My wounds are deeper than
anyone could ever see,
Without you, I am a skeleton,
I am no longer me.

You may see me,
But the I that I once was
now seizes to exist,
My soul lingers among
the interface between
where you have
gone and here, were
my body remains.

My heart is locked,
Only you have the key,
I will love you endlessly,
I will love you till the day
the very last grain of
salt leaves the sea.

I have loved,
And I have lost,
Now I sit alone,
I would give
anything to be
with you no
matter the cost.

How do I explain it to my heart,
When every time I walk into a room
my eyes still search for you.

I sit here silently,
As I continue to
bleed internally,
It is not that I
have nothing to say,
It is because no one
will understand anyway,
What is the use of
trying to explain,
When others will never
comprehend the
depth of my pain.

With you,
I was blind to see
how beautiful
the world was,
But I can clearly
see how ugly
it is without you.

This
would be our destiny,
This
would be our fate,
If I knew then,
What I know now,
I would still choose you,
Only you,
Over and over again.

Within these four walls,
Without any trace of light,
In other words,
Simply, a dark room,
This is my sanctuary,
Completely alone,
I sit silently,
This darkness conceals
my sadness,
So you cannot see,
The tears that
fall continuously.

There is no season or place
Where love cannot blossom or grow,
I will keep our love alive here,
And I know you will do the same there,
When I see you again, just how vast
our love is even God will know,
For he can forever walk in the
everlasting garden we did sow.

I have changed,
I am not the same,
Nor do I ever want to be,
The person who I once was,
Is not the me that you now see.

The person I was died the
same day that you were taken,
My world was turned upside down,
My life was completely shaken,
From this deep, dark disaster
I wish I could awaken.

I always thought
you would be close,
I always thought
you would be near,
No one have I loved more,
No one will ever be dear,
The thought of how
far you have gone,
And how you will
never return is always
followed by a tear.

And I know we would have
lasted forever,
If only this cruel world
had just let us be,
I know I would have
never left you,
And I know you would
have never left me.

I never knew existing would
be so exhausting now that I am alone,
My mind wanders and thinks of what
ifs and of the unknown,
When I miss you too much onto my
clothes I spray your cologne,
It does not smell the same on me,
And I am reminded once again that
you are gone.

My mind plays tricks on me,

I see you everywhere,

But I can never find you,

Have I gone mad,

Is this insanity?

As empty as I feel,
I should be as
weightless as a feather,
But this grief I
carry is so heavy,
It weighs me down,
I cannot move,
It is so surreal.

My once in a lifetime love,

my dearest friend,

You are my whole story,

My Beginning,

Middle

and End.

Do not tell me
that you understand,
The only way you
could is if you have felt it,
And if you have, you
are still going through it,
Grief is not an acquaintance
that is with you temporarily,
It is with you for your
entire life, it never leaves.

You always
shined the brightest,
That is why I know
you will always bring me light,
As I look up at the dark sky,
You are the brightest
star I see each night.

These are but words upon a page,
Inside of me there is chaos,
There is pain, agony and rage,
All I wish for is to be set free,
Life has locked me up in a cage.

The thought that you
will never be here
leaves me feeling
so very ill,
I have knots in
my stomach,
I feel frozen,
And there are
shivers down
my spine,
Lessen my misery,
Nothing can,
nothing ever will.

The day we are reunited,
There will be a glorious
rainbow in the sky,
It will be the most beautiful
thing in sight,
The angels will be happily
crying so there shall be rain,
The sun will shine so
radiant and bright,
It will be the day
there will finally be an
end to all my pain.

I am not living
Although I am alive,
The truth is without you,
I do not want to survive.

You used to start all
the poems you wrote
to me with roses are red,
violets are blue,
And without you now,
My world is completely
empty and colourless too.

Losing you,
The pain is relentless,
Thoughts of you,
Each time they come
they leave me breathless.

Day after day,
I awake in Hell,
How strange is it that
Hell looks exactly
like the world in
which we both
lived together,
The only difference
is that you are not here.

Married to this grief,
We have become one,
We will be together until
my last breath; til
death do us part.

When one door closes
another opens
Or, so I have heard,
The only door I am looking for
is the one that leads to you.

And because I
never got to
bid you farewell,
I know our story
is not yet over,
Our souls will be
drawn to eachother,
We will surely
meet in another
lifetime.

Meeting you once was all it took,
For me to realize that
you were the one,
I knew it was the kind of love
That could never be undone.

Days pass,
Weeks come and go,
Losing you is the most
pain my heart will
ever know,
With this pain is
the deepest sorrow,
For you will not
be present in
my tomorrow.

Azrael, Angel of Death,
I summon thee,
I have been waiting,
Waiting ever so patiently,
I stand here with arms wide open,
Come take me...

... Oh Azrael,
I beg of you, come give me
The freeing kiss,
Cannot you see, I do not want
to live,
Here, I do not want to be,
I cannot go on like this.

You will live forever,
I will immortalize you,
For what I write about our love,
Will always revive you.

I think about you always,
Each second of every minute
of every hour of everyday,
You are the first thing
I think about in the morning,
And the very last as my
tears put me to sleep,
You never truly know what love is,
Until it leaves you with
Wounds
This
Deep.

...

A Note from the Author

After the loss of my husband I had lost sense of self; I didn't know who I was without him. I chose to write poetry not only as a means of therapy, but as a way to connect with others who have gone through the same loss and also as a way to honour him in the only way I know how. I have been in love with poetry ever since I can remember and it has provided a way for me to express what I feel; feelings which are sometimes rather difficult to share vocally. Grief is universal. Grief is real. Grief is forever. I have experienced more lows than I ever had before but with the help of my family and friends I made it through the most difficult year of my life. With their encouragement I put this book together so others can have a

❋ ❋ ❋

glimpse into my reality and those who have gone through loss know that they are not alone. The only way to live with this grief is to live life to the fullest each day knowing that the people who we have lost only want what is best for us. So, live this life, for it is precious. We owe it not only to ourselves but also to the ones we love so dearly.

Thank you so much for purchasing my first book. If you would like to read more of my poetry and know about my future endeavours please follow me on Instagram @bygkaur.

All my love, gkaur

...

...

Manufactured by Amazon.ca
Bolton, ON